# THE CANADIAN BRASS
# 15 FAVORITE HYMNS
## EASY ARRANGEMENTS

### ARRANGED BY LARRY MOORE

**Using the Arrangements**

A music director/conductor can come up with various approaches to a hymn. For instance: verse 1 – no brass; verse 2 – brass (Standard Version); verse 3 – brass (Variation Verse); verse 4 – brass (Standard Version) with Trumpet Descant. Or, another example might be: verse 1 – brass (Standard Version) with keyboard; verse 2 – brass (Standard Version), no keyboard; verse 3 – brass (Variation Verse). Get creative!

**Optional Trumpet Descant**

The Conductor's Score also includes the part for a trumpet descant. The descant may be added to any of the Standard Version verses of a hymn. The trumpet part is available in the following Hal Leonard publication: 50485217 *The Canadian Brass: 15 Favorite Hymns–Trumpet Descants*

**Visit the official website of The Canadian Brass:**
www.canbrass.com

### HAL•LEONARD®
### CORPORATION
7777 W. BLUEMOUND RD. P.O. BOX 13819 MILWAUKEE, WI 53213

Visit Hal Leonard Online at
**www.halleonard.com**

Trombone 2

CANADIAN BRASS

# ALL CREATURES OF OUR GOD AND KING

Francis of Assisi
Trans. W.H. Draper

LASST UNS ERFREUEN

*Geistliche Kirchengesang*
Harmonized by Ralph Vaughan Williams

**STANDARD VERSION**
Joyously (♩ = 120)

* *rit.* is used only if the Variation Verse is played as the final verse

*Return to Standard Version as needed*

Trombone 2

**CANADIAN BRASS**
# ALL GLORY, LAUD, AND HONOR
## ST. THEODULPH

Theodulph of Orleans, ca. 820
Trans. by John Mason Neal, 1851; alt., 1859

Melchior Teschner, 1615

* *rit.* is used only if the Variation Verse is played as the final verse

*Return to Standard Version as needed*

Trombone 2

**CANADIAN BRASS**
# BLESSED ASSURANCE
**ASSURANCE**

Fanny J. Crosby

Phoebe P. Knapp

* *rit.* is used only if the Variation Verse is played as the final verse

*Return to Standard Version as needed*

Trombone 2

**CANADIAN BRASS**
# CHRIST THE LORD IS RISEN TODAY
**EASTER HYMN**

Charles Wesley

from *Lyra Davidica*, London, 1708

\* *rit.* is used only if the Variation Verse is played as the final verse

*Return to Standard Version as needed*

Trombone 2

**CANADIAN BRASS**

# COME, YE THANKFUL PEOPLE, COME

## ST. GEORGE'S, WINDSOR

Henry Alford

George J. Elvey

* *rit.* is used only if the Variation Verse is played as the final verse

*Return to Standard Version as needed*

Trombone 2

**CANADIAN BRASS**

# CROWN HIM WITH MANY CROWNS

DIADEMATA

Matthew Bridges, stanzas 1,2,4;
Godfrey Thring, stanza 3

George J. Elvey

* *rit.* is used only if the Variation Verse is played as the final verse

*Return to Standard Version as needed*

Trombone 2

**CANADIAN BRASS**

# FAIREST LORD JESUS
## (Beautiful Savior)
### CRUSADERS' HYMN

Anonymous German Hymn, *Munster Gesangbuch*, 1677;
translated, Source unknown, stanzas 1-3; Joseph A. Seiss, Stanza 4

*Schlesische Volkslieder*, 1842
arranged by Richard S. Willi[...]

*Return to Standard Version as neede[...]*

Trombone 2

CANADIAN BRASS

# FOR THE BEAUTY OF THE EARTH

DIX

Folliott S. Pierpoint, altered

Conrad Cocher;
arranged by William H. Monk

Trombone 2

**CANADIAN BRASS**
# GOD OF OUR FATHERS
**NATIONAL HYMN**

Daniel C. Roberts

George W. Warren

* *rit.* is used only if the Variation Verse is played as the final verse

*Return to Standard Version as needed*

Trombone 2

**CANADIAN BRASS**

# GUIDE ME, O THOU GREAT JEHOVAH
## (God of Grace and God of Glory)

William Williams;
translated by Peter Williams

CWM RHONDDA

John Hughes

\* *rit.* is used only if the Variation Verse is played as the final verse

*Return to Standard Version as needed*

Trombone 2

**CANADIAN BRASS**
# HOLY, HOLY, HOLY!
### NICEA

Reginald Heber

John B. Dykes

* *rit.* is used only if the Variation Verse is played as the final verse

*Return to Standard Version as needed*

**CANADIAN BRASS**

# JOYFUL, JOYFUL, WE ADORE THEE
## HYMN TO JOY

Trombone 2

Henry van Dyke

Ludwig van Beethoven

\* *rit.* is used only if the Variation Verse is played as the final verse

*Return to Standard Version as needed*

Trombone 2

**CANADIAN BRASS**
# LEAD ON, O KING ETERNAL
**LANCASHIRE**

Ernest W. Shurtleff

Henry T. Smart

* *rit.* is used only if the Variation Verse is played as the final verse

*Return to Standard Version as needed*

Trombone 2

**CANADIAN BRASS**

# A MIGHTY FORTRESS IS OUR GOD

**EIN FESTE BURG**

Martin Luther
Trans. by F.H. Hedge, based on Psalm 46

Martin Luther

* *rit.* is used only if the Variation Verse is played as the final verse

*Return to Standard Version as needed*

Trombone 2

**CANADIAN BRASS**

# O GOD, OUR HELP IN AGES PAST

## ST. ANNE

Isaac Watts;
based on Psalm 90

attr. William Croft

* *rit.* is used only if the Variation Verse is played as the final verse

*Return to Standard Version as needed*